West Africa

Ben Nussbaum

Consultants

Andrea Johnson, Ph.D.
Assistant Professor of History
California State University, Dominguez Hills

Maritha Osekre-Amey
Executive Director
Westfield Bridge College, Accra, Ghana

Brian Allman
Principal
Upshur County Schools, West Virginia

Publishing Credits

Rachelle Cracchiolo, M.S.Ed., *Publisher*
Emily R. Smith, M.A.Ed., *SVP of Content Development*
Véronique Bos, *Vice President of Creative*
Dani Neiley, *Editor*
Fabiola Sepulveda, *Series Graphic Designer*

Image Credits: p.8 Alamy/Robert Harding; p.10 Shutterstock/Amors photos; p.12 (top) Alamy/François-Olivier Dommergues; p.12 (bottom) Wiki Commons/Taguelmoust; p.13 Alamy/Incamerastock; p.14 Alamy/Chris Hellier; p.15 (top) Alamy/Omoniyi Ayedun Olubunmi; p.16 Alamy/Xinhua; p.17 Alamy/Pictorial Press Ltd; p.18 Alamy/Reuters; p.20 Getty Images/Boureima Hama/Stringer; p.22 Alamy/Hum Images; p.23 (top) Shutterstock/Delali Adogla-Bessa; p.23 (bottom) Alamy/Imagegallery2; p.32 Newscom/Luiz Rampelotto/ZUMA Press; all other images from iStock and/or Shutterstock

Library of Congress Cataloging-in-Publication Data

Names: Nussbaum, Ben, 1975- author.
Title: West Africa / Ben Nussbaum.
Description: Huntington Beach : Teacher Created Materials, Inc, 2023. |
  Includes index. | Audience: Ages 8-18 | Summary: "West Africa is
  changing, and it is growing. The continent is full of young people who
  will determine the future of the region. Discover West Africa's amazing
  history, stunning geography, and more"-- Provided by publisher.
Identifiers: LCCN 2022038403 (print) | LCCN 2022038404 (ebook) | ISBN
  9781087695150 (paperback) | ISBN 9781087695310 (ebook)
Subjects: LCSH: Africa, West--Juvenile literature.
Classification: LCC DT471 .N87 2023 (print) | LCC DT471 (ebook) | DDC
  916.6--dc23/eng/20220810
LC record available at https://lccn.loc.gov/2022038403
LC ebook record available at https://lccn.loc.gov/2022038404

Shown on the cover is Idanre Hill in Nigeria.

TCM
Teacher
Created
Materials

5482 Argosy Avenue
Huntington Beach, CA 92649
www.tcmpub.com
ISBN 978-1-0876-9515-0
© 2023 Teacher Created Materials, Inc.

Table of Contents

Changing West Africa

Change is everywhere in West Africa. The population is booming. Cities are growing. The economy is shifting. West Africa is very different today than it was a few decades ago.

Sixteen countries make up West Africa. The smallest is Cabo Verde. It is a group of islands. Mauritania, Mali, and Niger are the largest countries in West Africa. In all three, much of the land is desert. The other **landlocked** country in West Africa is Burkina Faso. Nigeria has the most people of any country in the region. Many of Africa's smallest countries are in West Africa. One of them is The Gambia. It is the smallest non-island country in Africa. Each country in the region has a unique history and culture. The geography varies as well. There are deserts and savannas. There are also **rain forests** and mountain ranges.

the island of Sal, Cabo Verde

Sahara Desert, Mauritania

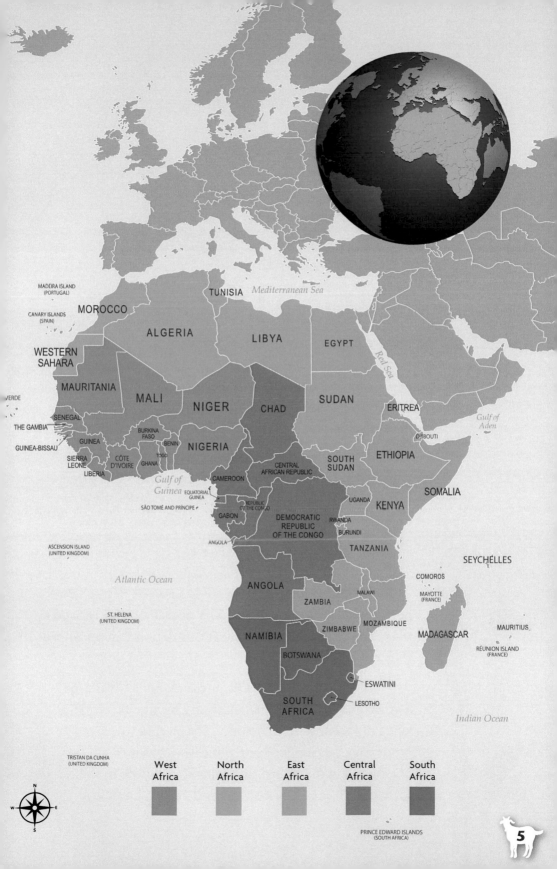

MADEIRA ISLAND
(PORTUGAL)

TUNISIA

Mediterranean Sea

MOROCCO

CANARY ISLANDS
(SPAIN)

ALGERIA

LIBYA

EGYPT

WESTERN
SAHARA

Red Sea

MAURITANIA

MALI

NIGER

CHAD

SUDAN

ERITREA

VERDE

*Gulf of
Aden*

SENEGAL

THE GAMBIA

DJIBOUTI

GUINEA-BISSAU

GUINEA

BURKINA
FASO

BENIN

NIGERIA

SOUTH
SUDAN

ETHIOPIA

SIERRA
LEONE

CÔTE
D'IVOIRE

TOGO

GHANA

SOMALIA

LIBERIA

CENTRAL
AFRICAN REPUBLIC

*Gulf of
Guinea*

CAMEROON

EQUATORIAL
GUINEA

UGANDA

KENYA

SÃO TOMÉ AND PRÍNCIPE

REPUBLIC
OF THE CONGO

GABON

DEMOCRATIC
REPUBLIC
OF THE CONGO

RWANDA

BURUNDI

ANGOLA

TANZANIA

SEYCHÉLLES

ASCENSION ISLAND
(UNITED KINGDOM)

Atlantic Ocean

COMOROS

ANGOLA

MALAWI

MAYOTTE
(FRANCE)

ZAMBIA

ST. HELENA
(UNITED KINGDOM)

MOZAMBIQUE

MADAGASCAR

MAURITIUS

ZIMBABWE

RÉUNION ISLAND
(FRANCE)

NAMIBIA

BOTSWANA

ESWATINI

LESOTHO

SOUTH
AFRICA

Indian Ocean

TRISTAN DA CUNHA
(UNITED KINGDOM)

West
Africa

North
Africa

East
Africa

Central
Africa

South
Africa

PRINCE EDWARD ISLANDS
(SOUTH AFRICA)

5

Sahara Desert,
Mauritania

West African Landscapes

The Sahara Desert stretches across a vast part of Africa, including parts of West Africa. There is no exact line where the desert ends. Instead, the desert slowly changes into different **terrain**. First, there are a few small plants across the land. Then, there is some grass and a few trees, followed by more and more greenery.

The Sahel is the name for the place where the Sahara first becomes a more livable area. It is dry and hot in the Sahel. In many places in the Sahel, months can pass without any rain. Then, there may be enough rain for grass and other plants to thrive for a few months.

In the past, Indigenous peoples survived in the Sahel by herding animals, such as goats or cows. They moved these animals to different locations depending on where they could find plants.

The Sahel gradually turns into a savanna. This area is a **grassland**. The savanna is too dry to allow for many kinds of farming. It is common for people to grow crops that can survive long periods without much rain. Sorghum and millet are two important grains in the savanna. They can be cooked and eaten like rice.

sorghum

African nomads in Mali

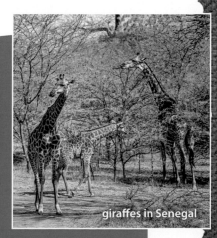

giraffes in Senegal

On Safari

Some of Africa's most well-known animals live in the savanna. This includes giraffes, elephants, lions, and leopards. Some people go on safaris to see them. They visit a national **preserve**. A guide takes visitors in a car or bus to see the animals. Serengeti National Park in East Africa is a famous place to see wildlife.

The savanna gradually turns into a lush, green rain forest near the coastline. These areas are famous for their **cacao** farms. Cacao beans are the main ingredient in chocolate. Côte d'Ivoire grows more cacao than any other country in the world.

Water sources play a big role in how people live in West Africa. The Niger River starts in the hills of the country of Guinea. It flows through Mali and Niger as well as other countries. It is important because it goes through areas that otherwise would not have much water.

An area in Mali is called the Inner Niger Delta. A delta is normally where a river meets another body of water. In a delta, a river splits into smaller streams to create swampy or marshy areas.

Farmers harvest cacao pods in Côte d'Ivoire.

fishers on the Niger River

The Inner Niger Delta is unusual because it occurs far from the sea. Instead, the Niger and many smaller rivers all flow through this area. For about four months a year, the whole region is very wet as the rivers flood. This is a period of abundant water. The water is vital for the people and the animals of the region.

crocodiles in Mali

The Niger River

The Niger is the third-longest river in Africa. The countries of Niger and Nigeria both take their name from this river. It is believed that this river was named by the Greeks. Many types of fish are found in the river. Crocodiles even live here!

The major lake of West Africa is Lake Chad. The countries of Niger, Nigeria, Cameroon, and Chad border this lake. Because it is shallow in parts, Lake Chad can grow or shrink quickly. This happens naturally when rainfall is high or low.

Lake Chad is important to this region. Many people depend on it for water. As more people get water from Lake Chad, it begins to dry up more quickly. Climate change is another part of the problem. Keeping Lake Chad healthy is complex. Many countries and people have to come to an agreement and all work together.

Lake Chad

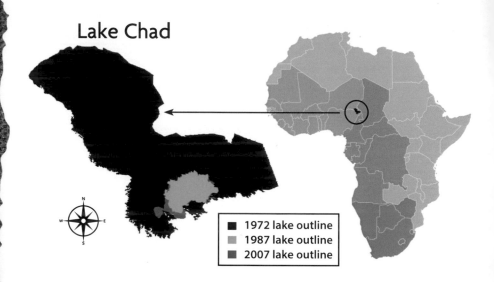

■ 1972 lake outline
■ 1987 lake outline
■ 2007 lake outline

Women gather water in Chad.

a Fulani boy with cows

Geography and Ethnic Groups

The geography of West Africa affects the ethnic groups who live there. Ethnic groups are people who speak similar languages and have shared customs. There are thousands of ethnic groups in Africa.

Ethnic groups tend to live in specific areas. For example, the Wolof live mostly in Senegal. Traditionally, they were farmers and lived in small, rural villages. Today, some of them are still farmers and have jobs in agriculture. But others moved to live in Dakar, the capital of Senegal. They work a variety of jobs.

The Fulani are another ethnic group. They traditionally live in the Sahel. Many Fulani are **herders**. They spend much of the year moving to new locations with their animals.

In the Depths

At its deepest, Lake Chad is about 35 feet (11 meters) deep. The largest lake in Africa is Lake Victoria. This lake goes through part of Uganda, Tanzania, and Kenya in East Africa. It is almost 300 feet (91 meters) deep.

Lake Victoria

ruins of the ancient Kingdom of Ghana in Mauritania

Vast History

Indigenous peoples have lived in West Africa for a very long time. Scientists are discovering human skeletons and tools that give hints of how Indigenous peoples lived many years ago. But there is a lot of guesswork. The details are hard to know.

The oldest West African kingdom that historians know a lot about was the Kingdom of Ghana. About 1,000 years ago, it controlled a large area in West Africa.

Eventually, Ghana faded. The Mali Empire came next. It built its wealth on trade between North Africa and West Africa. Salt and gold were the two most important parts of this trade.

Desert Salt

A large salt mine is in Mali. It has been in existence for at least 500 years. The area used to be a salty lake, but it is now a desert. Large **slabs** of salt are dug from under the ground. They are exported to other countries.

salt slabs in Mali

The most famous ruler of the Mali Empire was Mansa Musa. He followed the religion of Islam. An important part of the religion is a **pilgrimage** to Mecca. In 1324, Musa went to Mecca. This trip is famous. Stories about his trip were passed from one person to the next. Ancient historians also wrote about it. The trip showed the wealth of the Mali Empire. Musa traveled with 60,000 people. In front of Musa, 500 enslaved people carried gold staffs. The caravan included 80 camels loaded with gold. Everywhere he went, Musa gave away gold.

a map of the Western Sahara with Mansa Musa at the right

Eventually, the Mali Empire lost power. Smaller nations emerged. They were sometimes based around specific tribes. Some of these nations lasted for hundreds of years.

The Mande

The Mande are a group of people living in West Africa. They have been in the region for thousands of years. Between 4000 and 3000 BCE, the Mande independently developed the process of agriculture. Today, the Mande mostly live in western Sudan.

Dahomey warriors in the 1890s

Kingdom of Dahomey

A large kingdom existed in what is now Benin. It was called the Kingdom of Dahomey. It thrived from 1625 to 1894 CE. The government was a monarchy. Many kings ruled over the land. Women fought in battles. When they weren't fighting, they worked as bodyguards for the king.

The Igbo

The Igbo have lived in West Africa for thousands of years. Most of them were farmers. They grew various crops. Some of their staples were yams and taro. They also grew cassava. This could be turned into bread, flour, or other items. The Igbo had their own system of government. They had a village group. This was a group of villages with about 5,000 people total. The group shared a market space. They also had a shared meeting space. The leaders of the group were on a council. People were picked to be on this council through **lineage**. Today, the Igbo live mostly in southeastern Nigeria. They speak the Igbo language.

cassava

Independence

Some European countries used to control land in West Africa. In the 1500s, Portugal claimed what is now Guinea-Bissau. In the 1800s, Britain took areas that are now Nigeria and Ghana. In 1895, France took a large part of West Africa as its **colony**. Germany had a small colony around Togo in the late 1800s.

This period of time had a major impact. In West Africa, and on the whole continent, colonizers did not treat Africans well. They forced some people into jobs they did not want. Wealth from these African nations flowed to Europe. After World War II, West African countries started to gain more freedom. This was a step toward independence.

parade on Ghana's 61st independence anniversary

Kwame Nkrumah

One hero of African independence was Kwame Nkrumah. He started a **political** party in Ghana. The party supported independence. The party became popular. Nkrumah became popular, too. He won an election. He became a member of the government, even though it was controlled by Britain. Nkrumah led Ghana to independence without a war. In 1957, Ghana became its own country. Nkrumah was its first prime minister.

In other countries, West Africans fought for their independence. Many people died. By 1975, all of West Africa was independent.

Liberia

Only one West African country was never under colonial rule. This was Liberia. This country was founded by freed enslaved people from the United States. A group called the American Colonization Society sent them back to Africa. The colony was founded in 1821. It became known as Liberia in 1824.

Jobs and Industries

Hollywood in the United States is one of the main centers of the global movie industry. West Africa has its own version of Hollywood. Because it is in Nigeria, it is called *Nollywood*. Nollywood movies are popular all over Africa. They are also popular with other people who live around the world. It is estimated that more than one million people work in Nollywood. It is a thriving, growing part of the economy of West Africa.

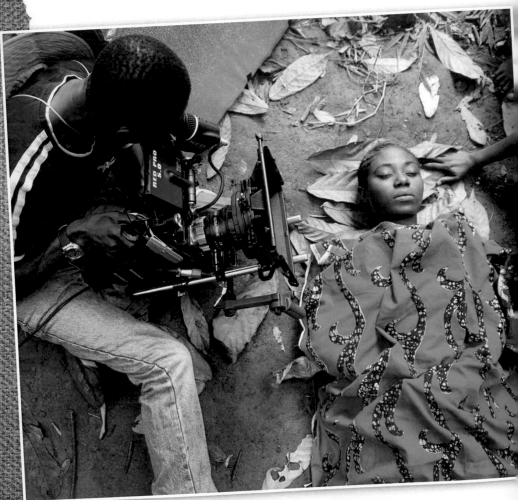

A film crew works on the movie *October 1* in Nigeria.

henhouse in Nigeria

Other industries make up the economy as well. Most West Africans are farmers. **Subsistence farming** is very common. Subsistence farmers eat most of the food they grow. At times, they may not have any food at all left to sell. These farmers grow lots of different kinds of food. For example, a farmer might raise goats and grow vegetables and millet. The goats provide meat and milk. The vegetables provide **nutrients**. The millet is a staple of most meals. So, subsistence farmers usually do not have to buy any food at all.

Larger farms in West Africa are focused on one or two crops. The workers here are paid to harvest crops. Cacao farming is one example. West Africa also produces a lot of peanuts, palm oil, and cotton.

Popular Dishes

Fufu is a dough-like food that is eaten with stews. It is made out of a boiled starch, such as cassava. The cassava is then pounded for a long time. It is formed into a ball. *Garri* is a different type of processed cassava. *Maafe* is a type of peanut stew from Mali. It includes meat that is cooked in a sauce of tomatoes, onions, and peanut butter.

fufu
garri

19

People search for gold in Niamey, Niger.

Gold mining is an important part of the economy in West Africa. Some large mines are owned by big companies. Miners work for them and use large machines and tools. But some miners work for themselves. They mine gold on their own land with simple tools. This type of mining is a very old tradition in West Africa. Other types of minerals and metals are mined in the region, too. Niger has deposits of the rare metal uranium. Uranium is used in nuclear power plants. These metals and minerals are exported to other countries.

A major source of wealth in West Africa is oil. Nigeria has rich oil deposits. Much of the oil is in the area where the Niger River enters the sea. Oil is one reason why Nigeria has the potential to be a huge economic power. This resource can be exported for a profit. Another reason for Nigeria's potential economic power is its large population. More than 200 million people live in Nigeria. No other country in West Africa comes close to that.

Nigerian leaders have also been focused on building better **infrastructure**. This refers to structures such as roads, bridges, and ports. These improvements will help grow its economy. They could bring in more tourism, too.

An oil rig in Nigeria extracts oil from under the seafloor.

Marketplaces

There are several busy markets in major West African cities. The Makola Market in Ghana has existed for decades. It is an open-air market that is filled with goods, including clothing, produce, and other products. Balogun Market in Nigeria also has clothing and shoes for sale. People who come to the market can purchase food and snacks, too.

Progress and Change: Civics

Most governments in West Africa are republics. This means that citizens elect their leaders. Each country has a constitution. It describes the structure of the government. It also describes the laws.

Voting in elections allows the people of a country to have a say in their governments. But some places in West Africa have run into issues. In 2017, a new president of The Gambia was elected fairly. But the old president did not want to leave office. After a few tense days, he fled to another country.

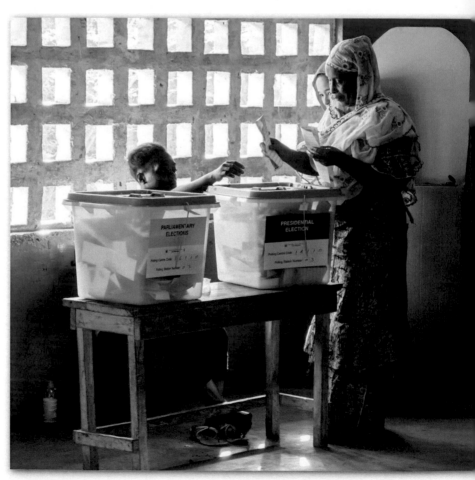

A woman in Sierra Leone votes in the presidential election.

Ghana's Parliament

Sometimes, politics in this region involves **tension** or rivalries between ethnic groups. All the countries of West Africa have a diverse mix of ethnic groups. In one presidential election, a member of the Kru ethnic group and a member of the Mande group ran against each other. It was a very close election. The member of the Mande group lost by a small amount. It led to a war between the northern part and southern part of Côte d'Ivoire.

Political conflict has been common in West Africa. But some countries are making changes. Sierra Leone and Ghana are leading the way. These countries have had free and fair elections.

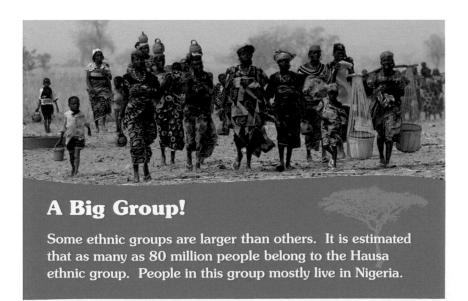

A Big Group!

Some ethnic groups are larger than others. It is estimated that as many as 80 million people belong to the Hausa ethnic group. People in this group mostly live in Nigeria.

23

Climate change is also an issue that affects West Africans. In some places, the desert is growing. This is called **desertification**. For example, the Sahara is steadily growing. A report showed that it has grown 10 percent since 1920. It has pushed into the Sahel in some places. Areas that had been useful for farming are drying out because of it.

Desertification can happen for several reasons. Drought and **deforestation** are factors. Little or no rain prevents an area from getting moisture. And as the desert grows, people have to move out of that area. This makes the population of other areas quickly grow. That means too many people have to live in small cities or towns. This can create tension.

Plants that cover the ground in the northern part of Senegal dry up during the dry season.

Some steps are being taken to solve these problems. In West Africa, there is a group called the Economic Community of West African States (ECOWAS). This is a group made of different West African countries. In May 2022, the group came to an agreement. They made a strategy to address global warming over the next 10 years. This will include spending money to address issues and raising awareness.

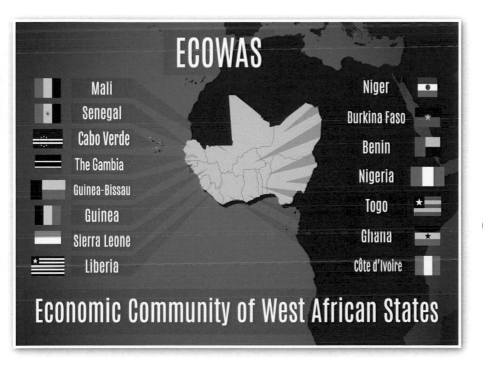

A Global Problem

Growing deserts are a problem in many places. This includes the western United States and large parts of Australia. Countries in central Asia, such as Kazakhstan, are facing this problem, too. Some countries have made international agreements to address issues like this. The Paris Agreement is one example.

Into the Future

West Africa's long history can be seen throughout the region. Many museums tell the stories of the past. The people living in this region tell the story of the present. And many changes underway tell the story of the future. Africa's largest oil refinery is being built in Nigeria. It will transform Nigeria's oil industry. A **redevelopment** is underway in Accra, Ghana. A massive project called the Marine Drive Project will redesign a section of beachfront land. The goal is to increase tourism to Ghana. Thousands of jobs will be created, too.

In Lagos, the biggest city in Nigeria, a new port is being built. Huge cargo ships will be able to quickly load and unload. Off the coast of Senegal, a giant project is building technology to mine gas under the seafloor. Railways, airports, and highways are being built. Mobile technology continues to improve, too. In the past, there was a lack of infrastructure. But that has changed. In the early 2000s, cell phones increased in popularity. They allowed Africans to have greater access to services, such as banking and health care.

What kind of place will West Africa be in 10 years? Only time will tell. The young people of West Africa will make the future. And the future of West Africa looks bright.

How Young Is Young?

West Africa has many young people. The median age of a person in Mali is about 16. Birth rates are high in some West African countries. More young people means an increased need for certain resources. Education is a key resource. Young West Africans need to have access to all levels of schooling. They also need to have access to entry-level jobs. According to a United Nations report, those are two of the biggest issues for young West Africans.

A container ship passes by Eko Atlantic, a new coastal city by Lagos, Nigeria.

Map It!

The Niger River is very important in West Africa. It is an important source of water for people, animals, and plants. Make a map to show the path of the Niger River and other rivers of the region.

1. Start by making a map of the West African countries. Label each country.

2. Trace the path of the Niger River on your map. Label any major cities on or near the river.

3. Label the delta of the river. Also, include the Inner Niger Delta. This is the area in Mali that floods each year when the Niger River is high.

4. Add the Senegal River, Volta River, Bani River, and Benue River to your map.

the Niger River

the Volta River

Niger River

● Timbuktu

● Bamako

● Niamey

Lokoja ●
Asaba ●

Fulani people prepare to
cross the Bani River in Mali.

29

Glossary

cacao—a type of tree that grows cacao beans, the main ingredient in chocolate

colony—an area that is controlled by or belongs to a distant country

deforestation—the action of clearing or removing all trees from an area

desertification—the process of land becoming desert

grassland—an area of land with few trees or bushes that is covered in tall grass

herders—people whose job it is to herd animals

infrastructure—the system of public works in an area, such as roads and bridges

landlocked—shut in or enclosed by land on all sides

lineage—descent in a line from a common ancestor

nutrients—substances that help people, animals, or plants grow and be healthy

pilgrimage—a journey to a special place, usually for religious reasons

political—relating to politics or government

preserve—a protected area for animals or plants

rain forests—woodland areas with a high annual rainfall and very tall trees, often found in tropical regions

redevelopment—renovation of an area

slabs—thick pieces

subsistence farming—a system of farming that provides enough crops for one person's or one family's needs

tension—a state of unfriendliness

terrain—land

a Tuareg village in Niger

Index

Learn More!

Ellen Johnson Sirleaf was the president of Liberia from 2006 to 2018. She was the first woman to be elected as a leader of an African country. She won the Nobel Peace Prize in 2011. Research Sirleaf. Pretend you are awarding her with the Nobel Peace Prize. Create a speech that lists her accomplishments and why she deserves the Nobel Peace Prize. Be sure to answer these questions:

- What was her career like?

- Why did Sirleaf spend time in the United States in the 1960s?

- Why did she have to leave Liberia in 1980?

Monrovia, Liberia